LONDON UNDERGROUND 1970-1980

In the series *Vintage Britain*

LONDON UNDERGROUND 1970–1980

MIKE GOLDWATER

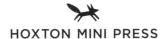

HOXTON MINI PRESS

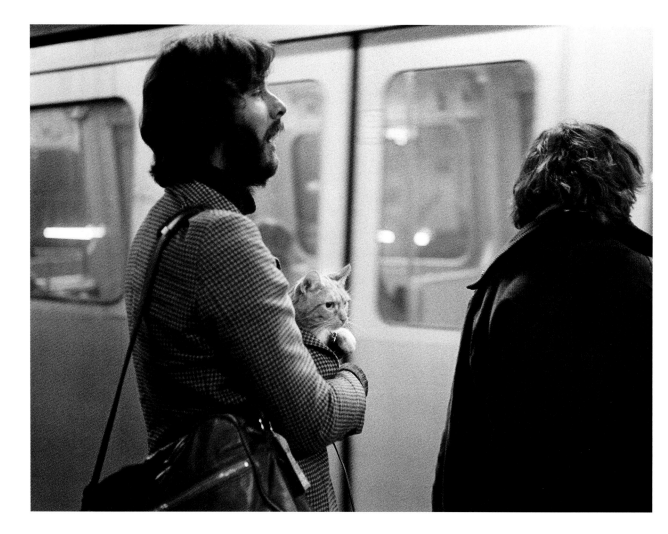

INTRODUCTION

Stand at Angel or Barons Court or Temple stations and beneath your feet – beneath the tarmac and the centuries-weathered stone, in the seams of sand and gravel and clay extending under London – millions of people will be hurtling through the black.

Down here, beyond the wind and rain, away from birdsong, tree-leaves and light, the 11 lines of the capital's Underground railway unravel across the city; all the way from the heaving scramble of its middle, to its quiet outreaches, spidering east and west along the Thames.

Since it opened in 1863, this vast and rambling network (famously simplified by Harry Beck's diagrammatic map of 1933), has engendered its own half-world. Descend into it and you are neither here nor there, only in-between.

In its confined curved spaces, sound reverberates and magnifies. The growl or roar of a distant train, the grinding and clanking of brakes. The comforting litany of announcements: Mind the gap. Stand clear of the doors. Half-remembered sequences of station names on a line. Trains that are there one minute and gone the next.

Barge your way aboard and watch the platform appear to liquefy, sliding past the glass pane as the train accelerates. There's a thrill in the rush through a tunnel, particularly if you stand by the open window at the front of the carriage.

It's a world in which you are oddly insulated and invisible: entirely alone, despite the crowds, which part and close, in a restless ebb and flow. As early as 1906, the author John Galsworthy describes Soames Forsyte's fellow travellers on the underground as 'shadowy figures, wrapped each in his own little shroud of fog, [they] took no notice of each other'.

Mike Goldwater began taking pictures on the Underground in 1970. Having grown up in a north London suburb, from where he travelled the

Northern line to school in Hampstead (the deepest station on the network, he and his friends would compete to run fastest down its 320-step spiral staircase) Goldwater was already familiar with the Tube, though it was quite different from the one we know today.

Back then, you had to buy your ticket from a window and show it at the barrier. The advertisements on the wall were unabashedly sexist. You could puff undisturbed on a cigar and tap your ash on the carriage floor. Some stations were lit only by individual hanging bulbs in white light shades, immersing travellers in a dim, Hades-like gloom. It made taking photographs incredibly difficult, forcing Goldwater to function at the very limit of his film's capabilities, but it gives his pictures a wonderfully brooding, unearthly cast. He had to hide his camera from Underground staff, who would stop him taking pictures if they caught him.

Walker Evans famously concealed his camera from New York's underground commuters when he photographed them between 1938 and 1941, but though Goldwater's subjects were sometimes unaware of him taking a picture, he avoided subterfuge with the passengers if he could. He was helped by the fact that most people on the Underground are completely absorbed in getting to their destination as quickly as possible. Meanwhile, Goldwater had no destination at all: he'd climb on and off trains, change lines, stop for a moment in booking halls and tunnels, but he was always set apart; the discreet onlooker, sensitive to the grand gestures and minor details of life as it unfolded before his camera. It is a measure of his skill that the photographs often seem like staged tableaux, especially in the way the figures are positioned. Each shape, shadow and outline has a role.

At busy times, the way in which people negotiate and preserve their modicum of space when they are forced into close proximity often made for interesting pictures. He watched particularly for any quirky interactions. A snatched kiss, a conversation. A yawn, a sly glance. People who are tired, people who are drunk, people who are lost in thought. Match days and rush hours were a goldmine, but so were lone travellers on empty platforms. Little flashes of familiarity – with the children dancing in a nearly empty carriage, for instance, and the desolate teenage football fans near the Arsenal, after Man United lost the Cup Final in May 1979 – was one of his rewards. Goldwater often wondered if the same intense encounters would take place above ground, or whether they could only ever happen under it.

For 10 years, as his career began to take shape, Goldwater continued his underground wanderings. All the while, trouser legs narrowed, lapels shrunk, buskers continued to flout the law, new lines opened and others were extended, passenger numbers grew.

Goldwater's series ends in 1980, when he joined forces with seven other photographers to form the cooperatively-owned picture agency, Network Photographers, drawing his Underground series to a close. It means that the pictures present a neatly contained moment in time, the Tube travellers forever preserved, resisting the impermanence that marks out their underground setting.

Lucy Davies
London, 2019

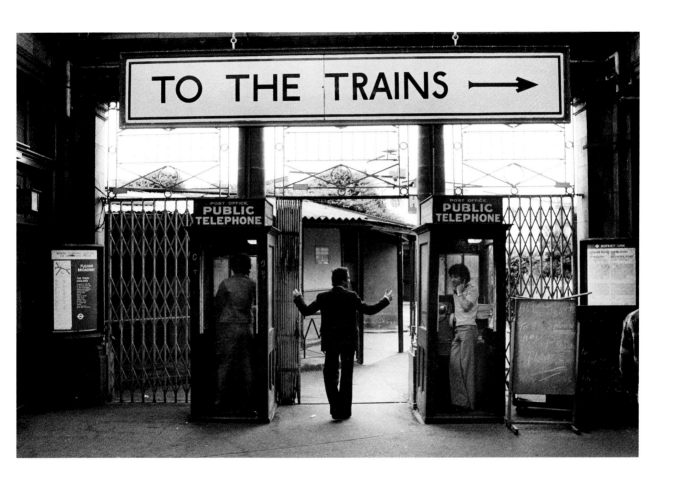

Fulham Broadway, 1979

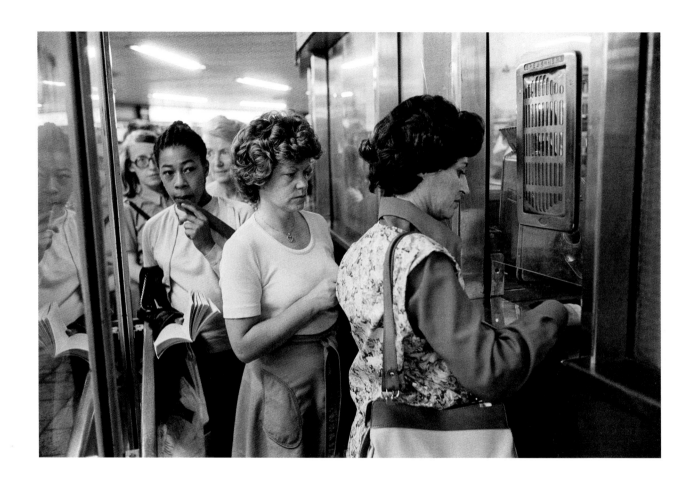

Oxford Circus, 1979

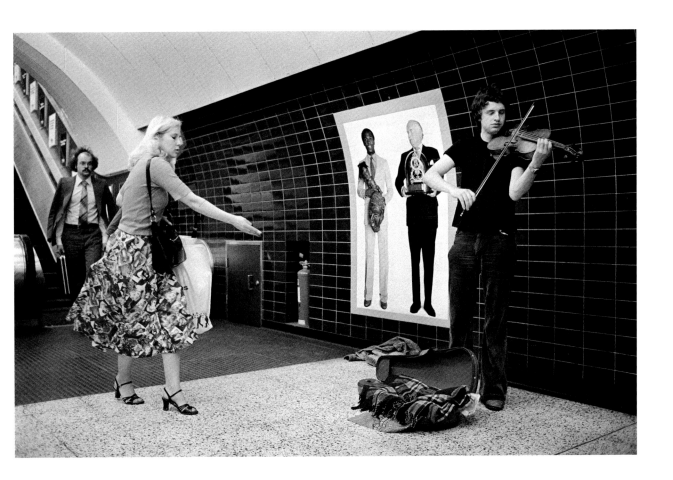

Holborn, 1979

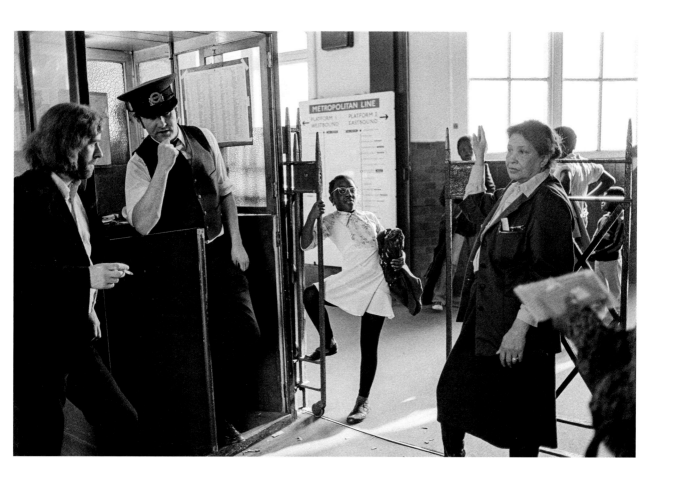

Westbourne Park, 1979

Baker Street, 1980

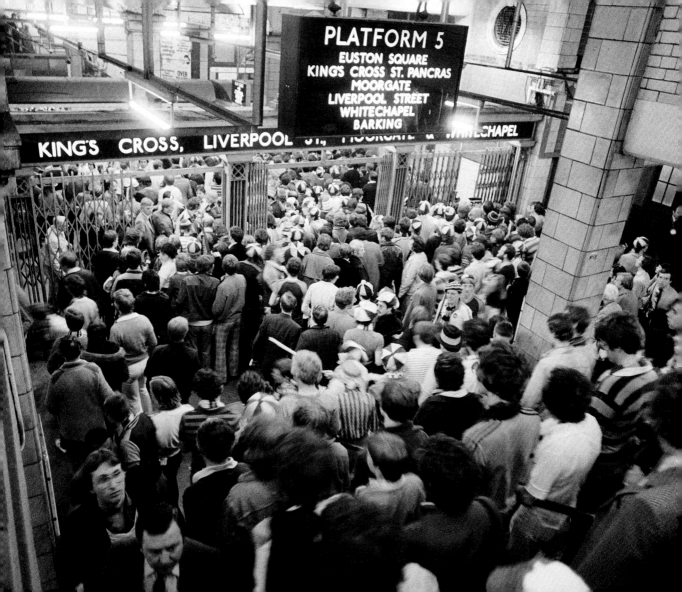

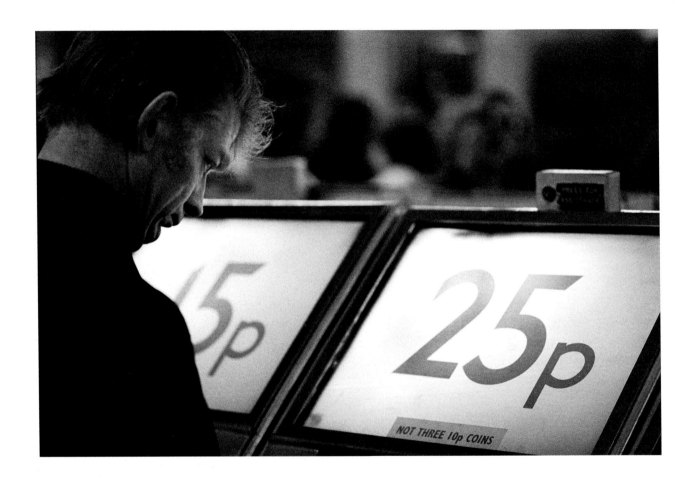

NOT THREE 10p COINS

Piccadilly Circus, 1978

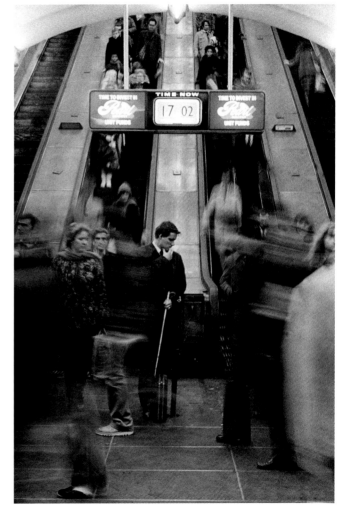

Holborn, 1979

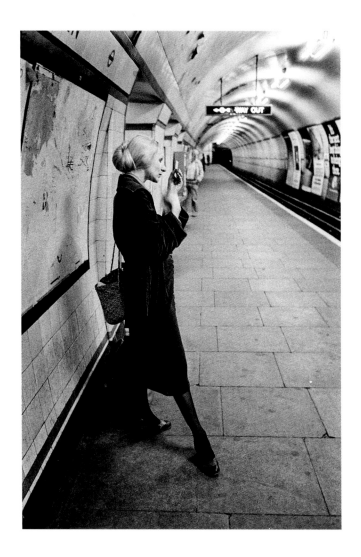

Chalk Farm, 1980

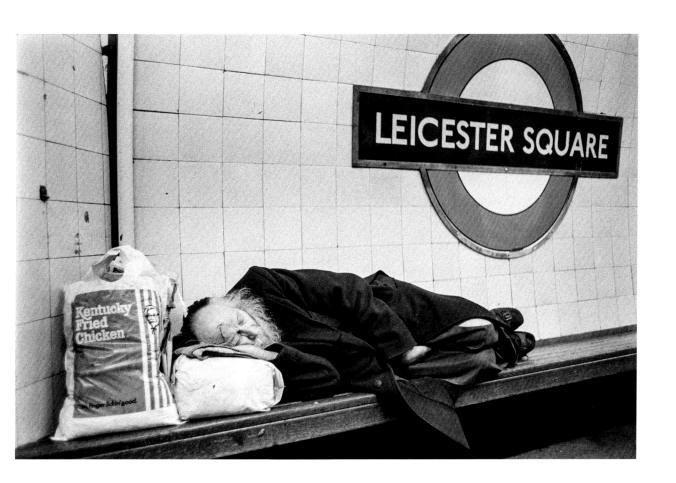

Leicester Square, 1973

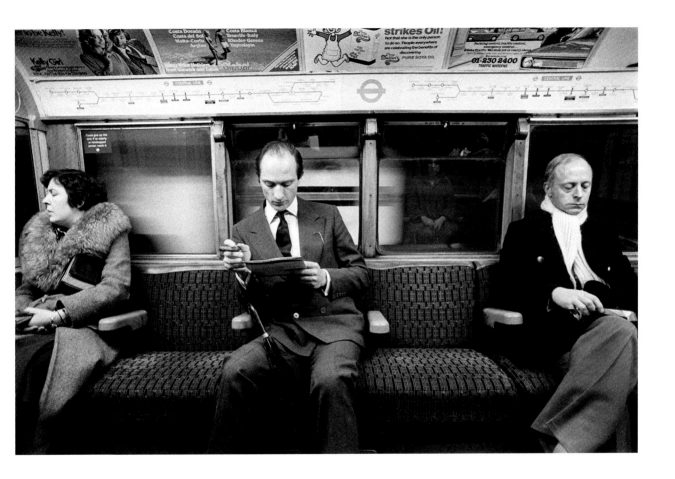

Central Line, 1978

Northern Line, 1979

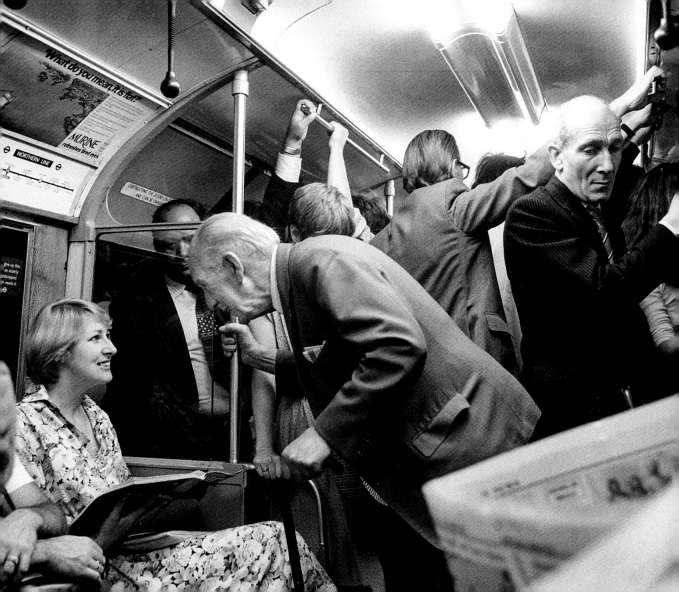

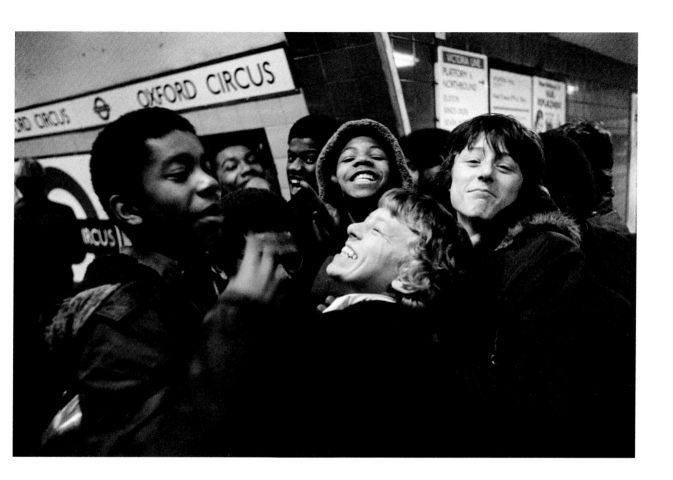

Oxford Circus, 1978

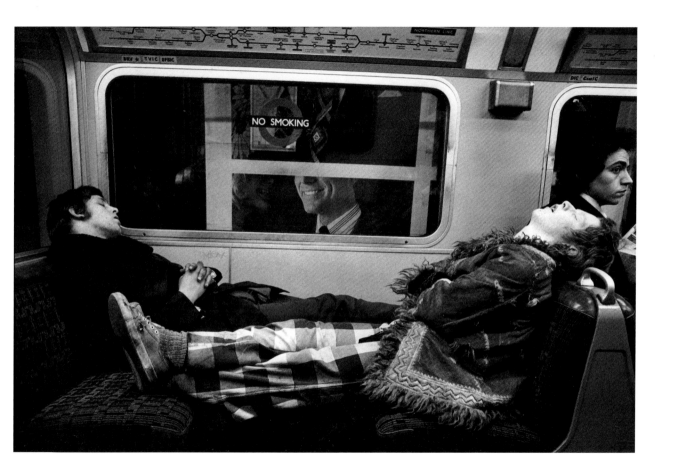

Northern Line, 1975

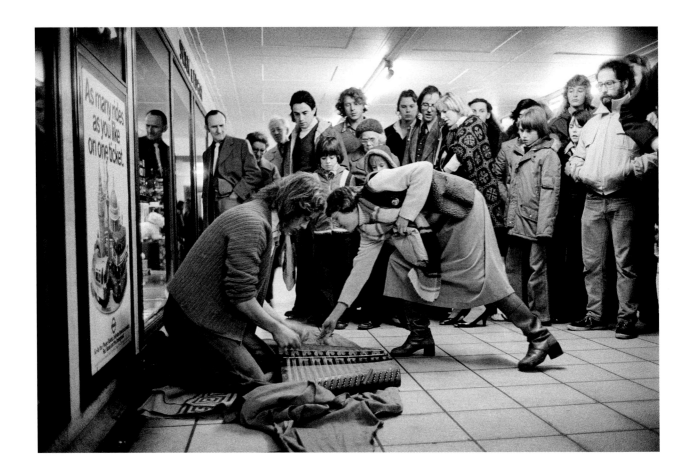

Piccadilly Circus, 1978

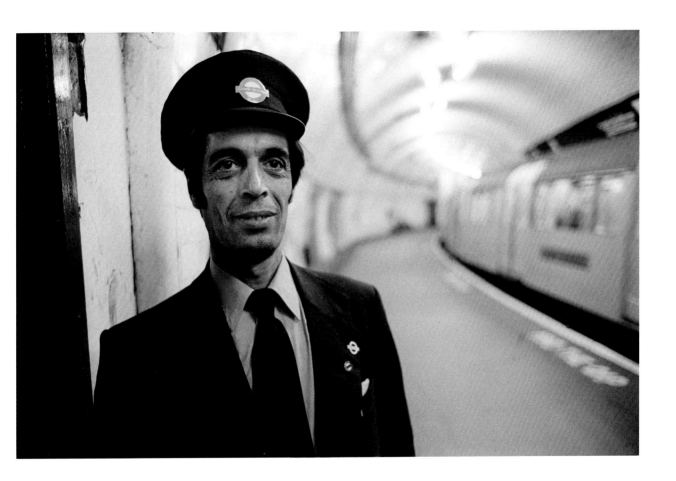

Bank, 1979

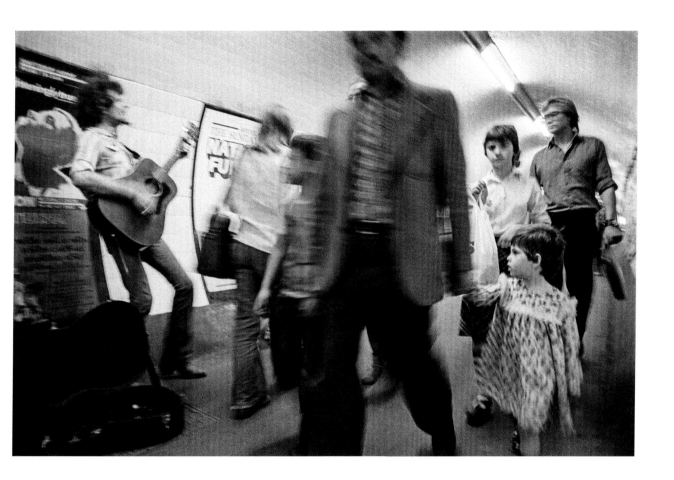

Bank, 1979

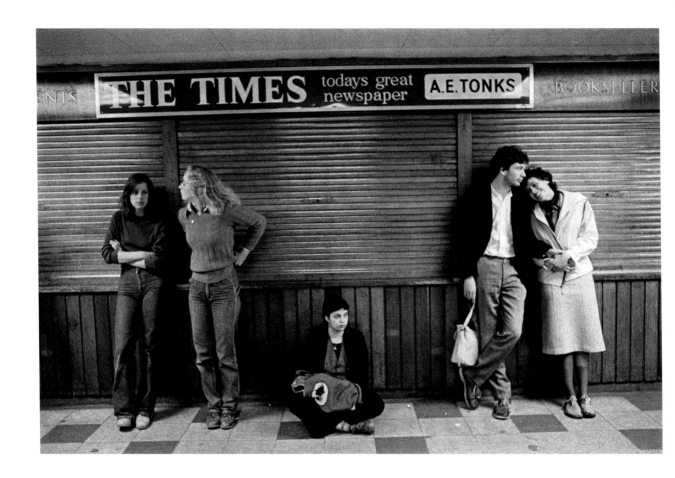

Notting Hill Gate, 1979

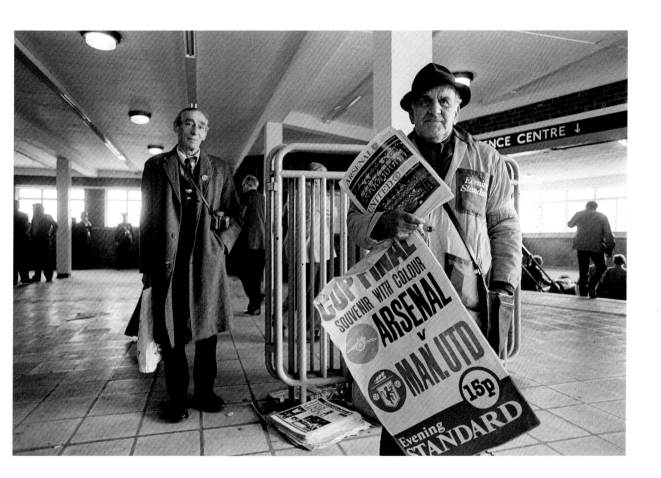

Wembley Park, 1979

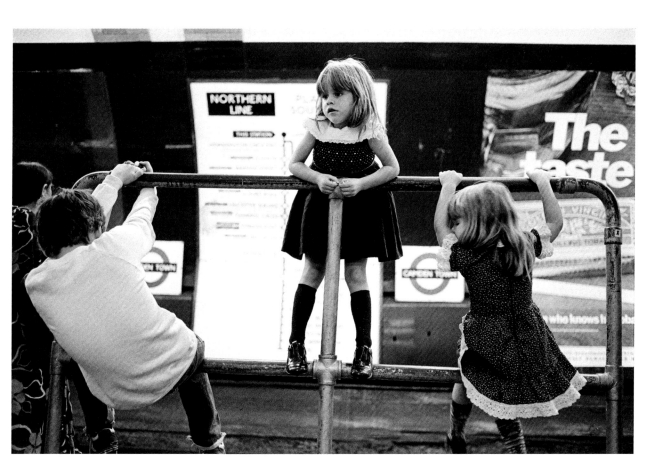

Camden Town, 1979

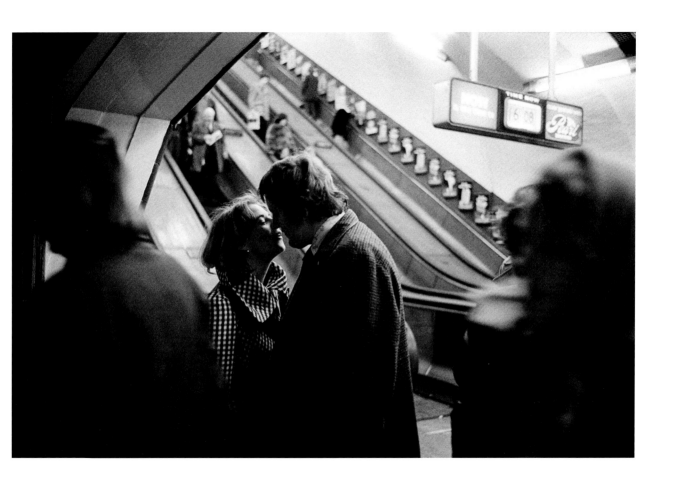

Holborn, 1978

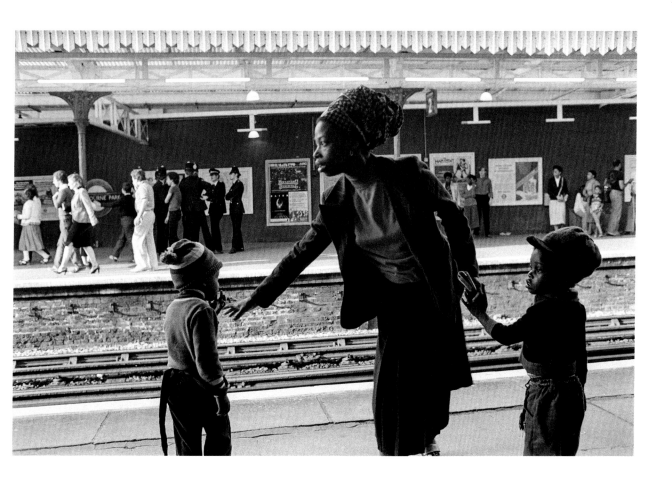

Westbourne Park, 1979

Farringdon, 1978

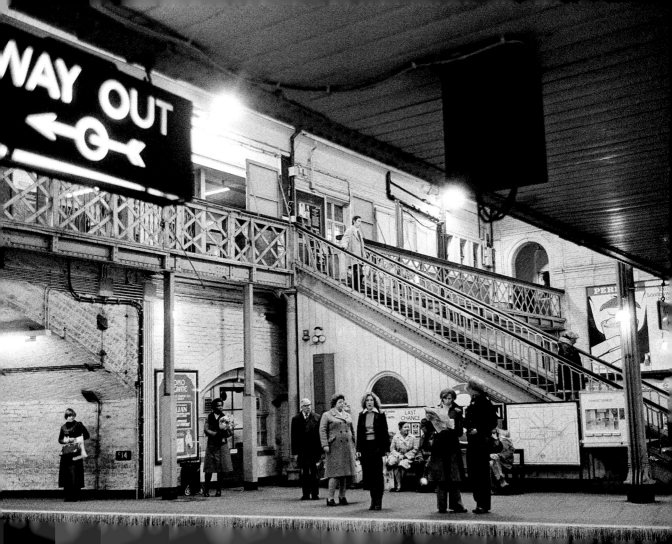

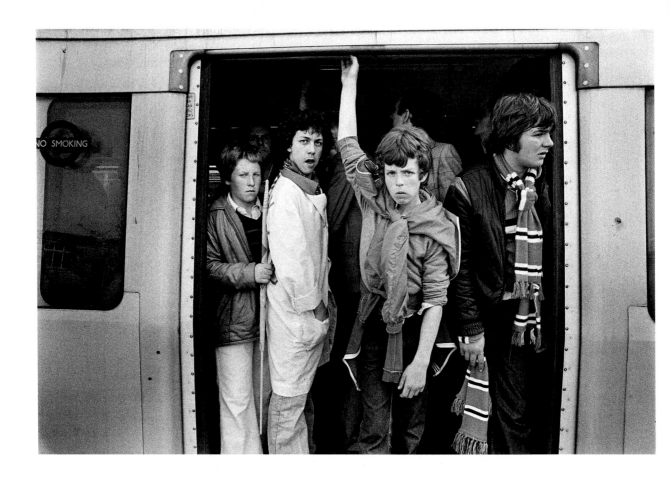

Wembley Park, 1979

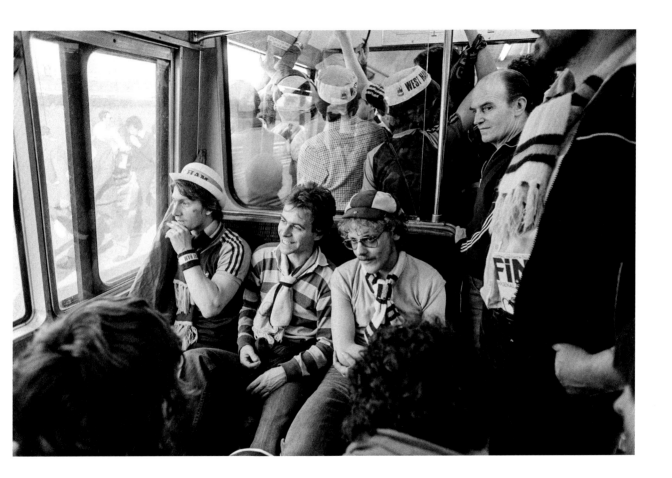

Metropolitan Line, 1980

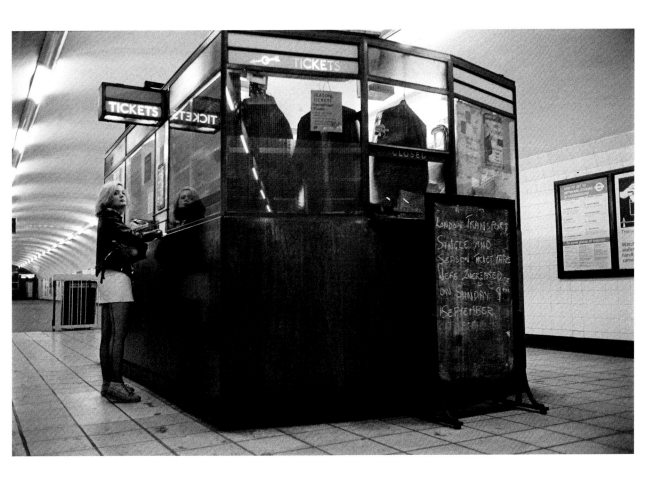

King's Cross, 1979

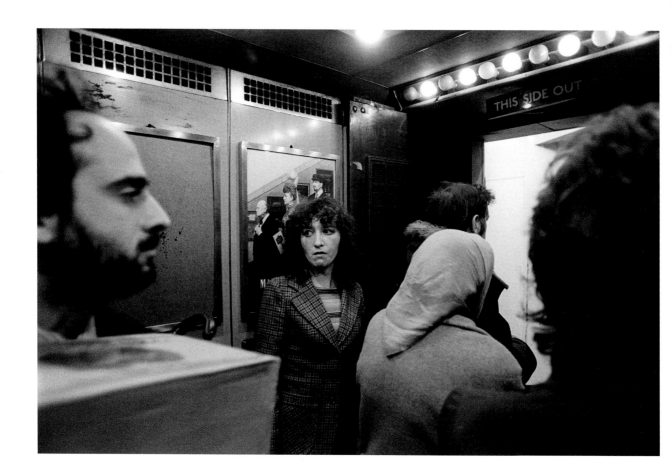

Goodge Street, 1979

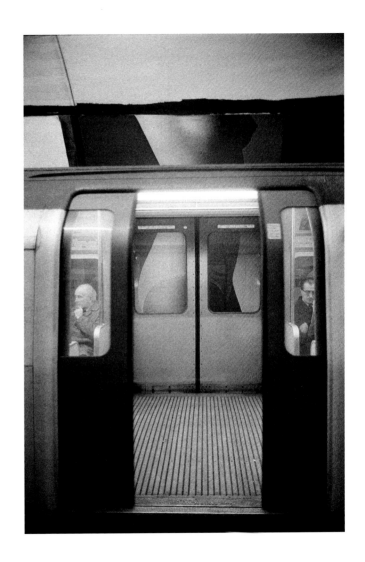

Oxford Circus, 1978

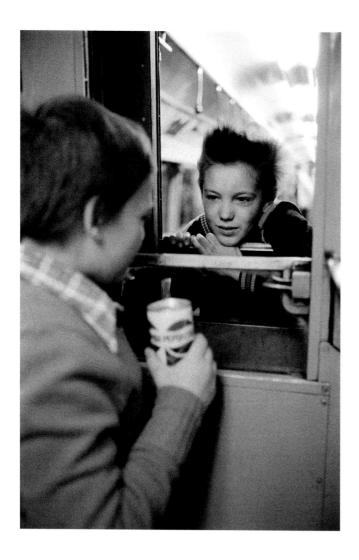

Northern Line, 1980

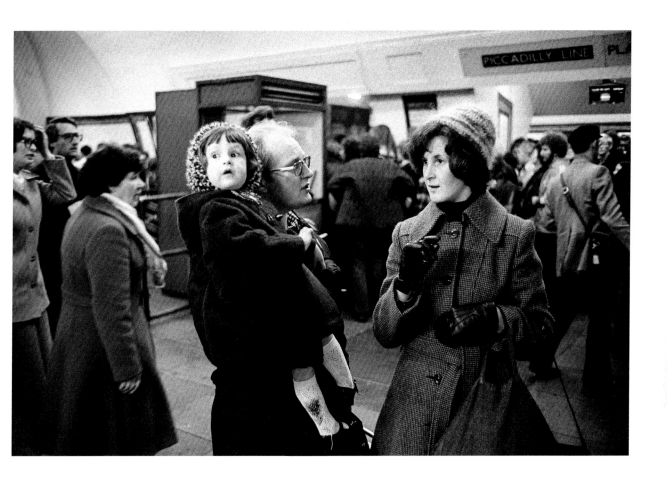

Piccadilly Circus, 1978

Notting Hill Gate, 1978

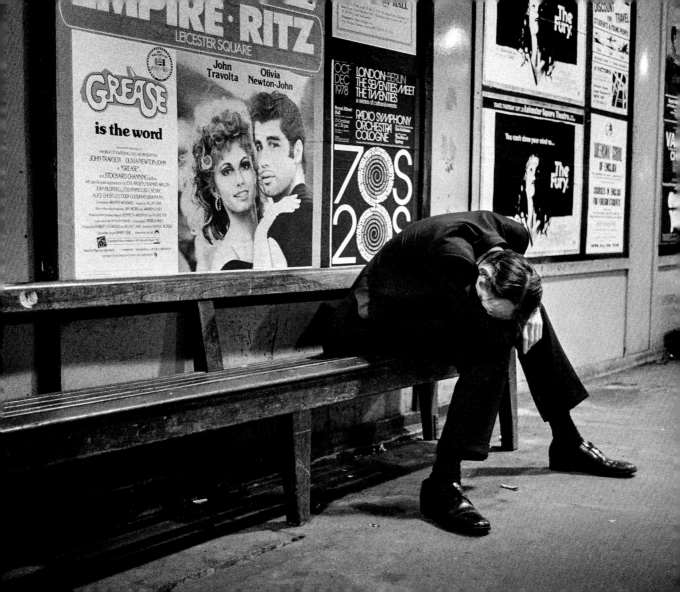

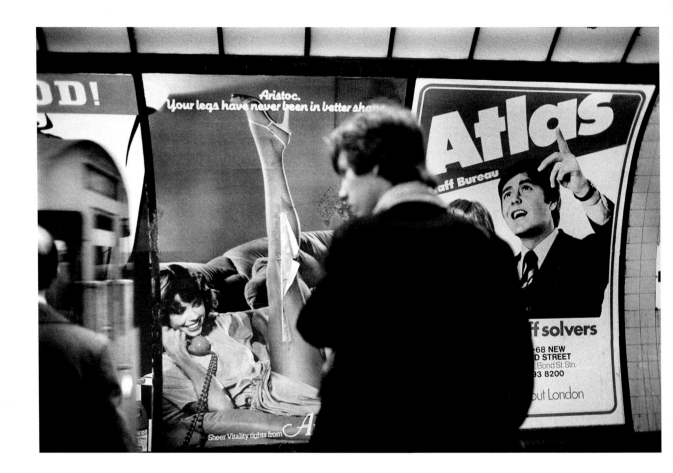

Oxford Circus, 1979

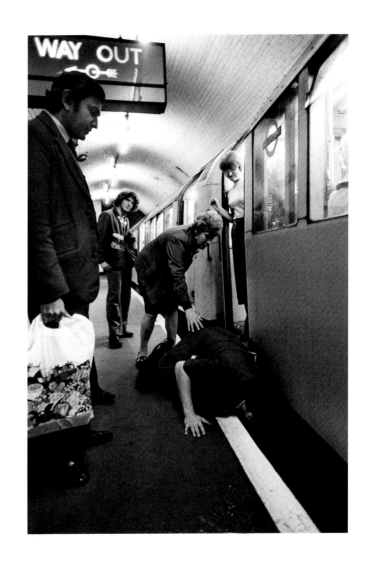

Bank, 1979

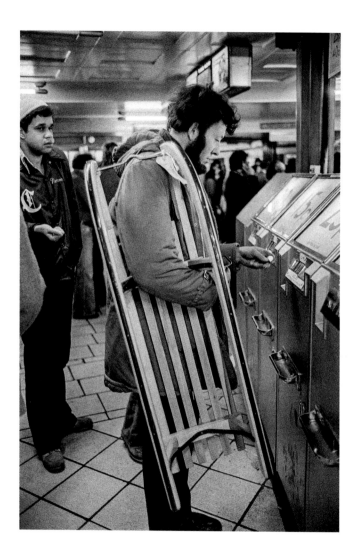

Piccadilly Circus, 1978

District Line, 1979

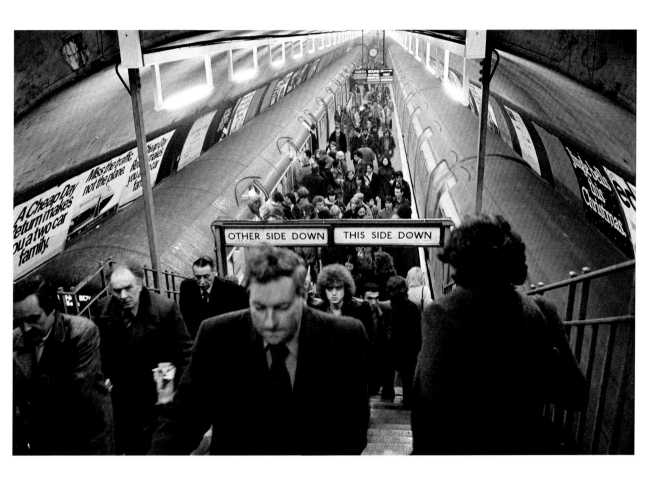

Angel, 1979

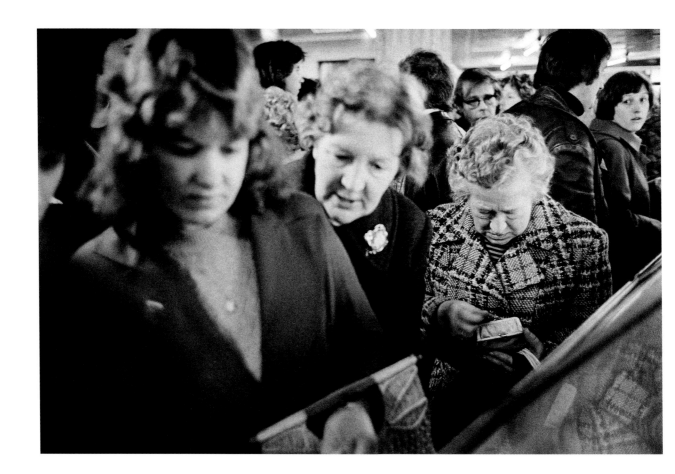

Piccadilly Circus, 1978

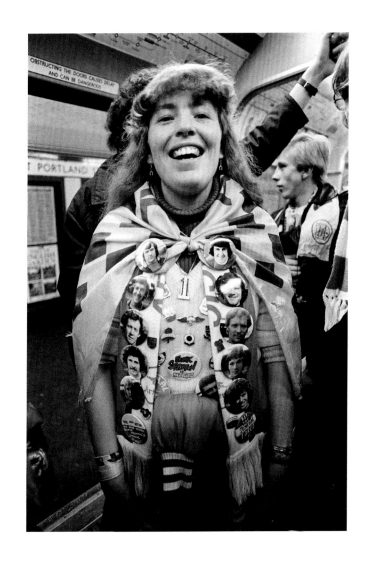

Great Portland Street, 1979

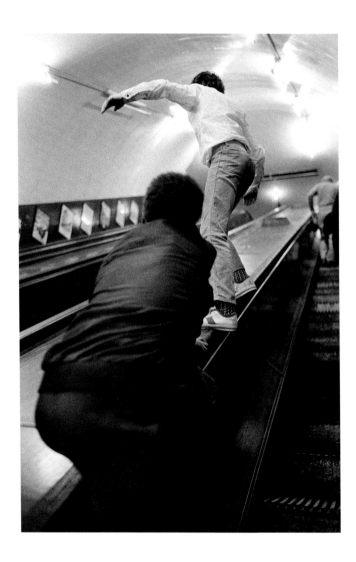

Bank, 1978

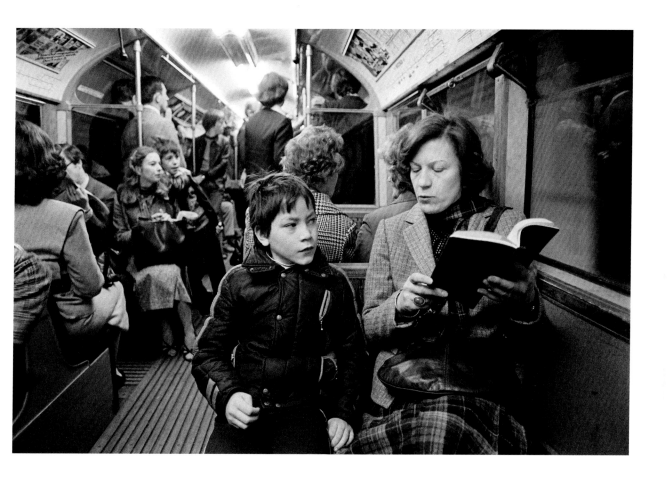

Central Line, 1980

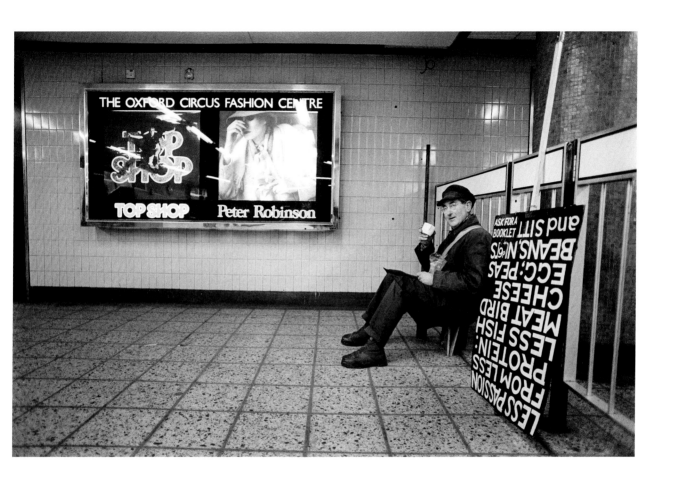

Oxford Circus, 1979

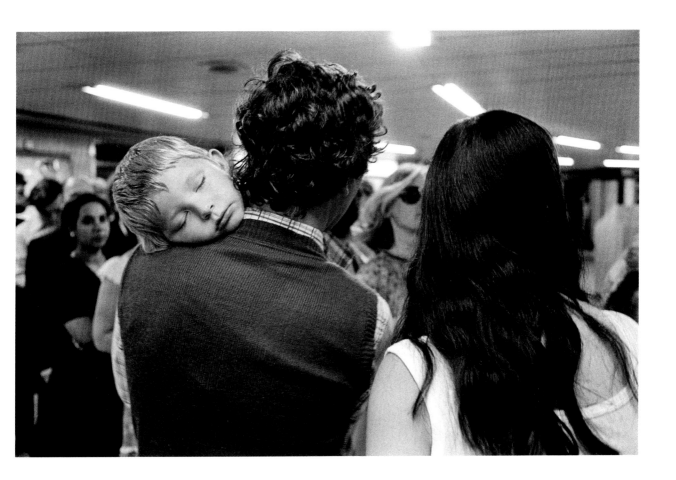

Oxford Circus, 1979

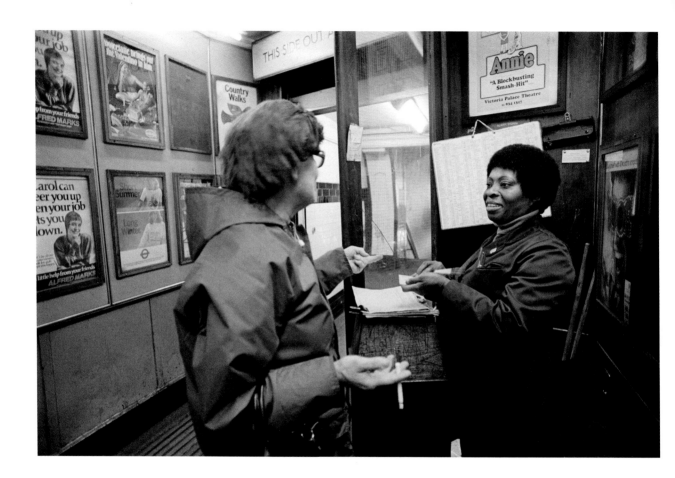

Aldwych, 1979

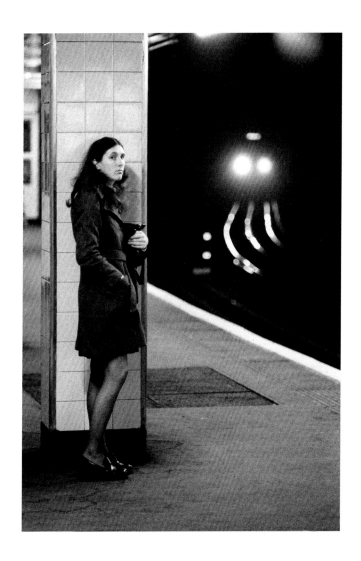

Moorgate, 1973

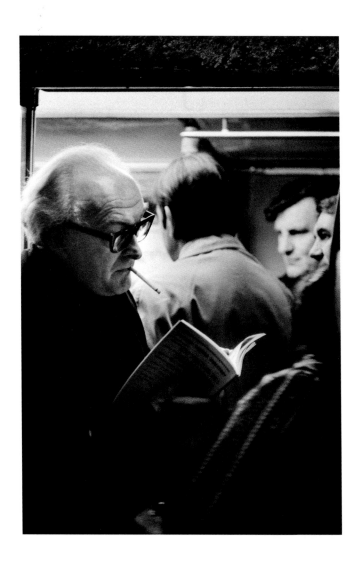

Piccadilly Line, 1974

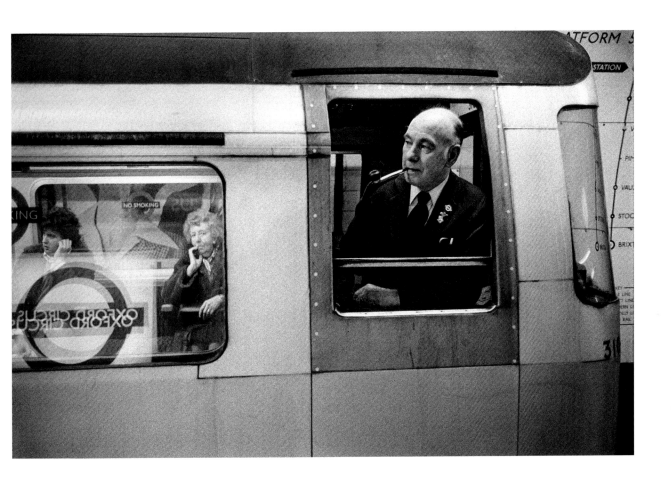

Oxford Circus, 1978

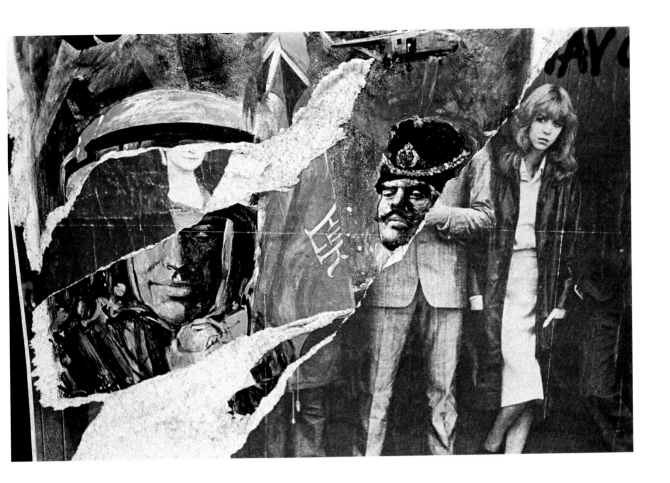

Bank, 1979

Northern Line, 1974

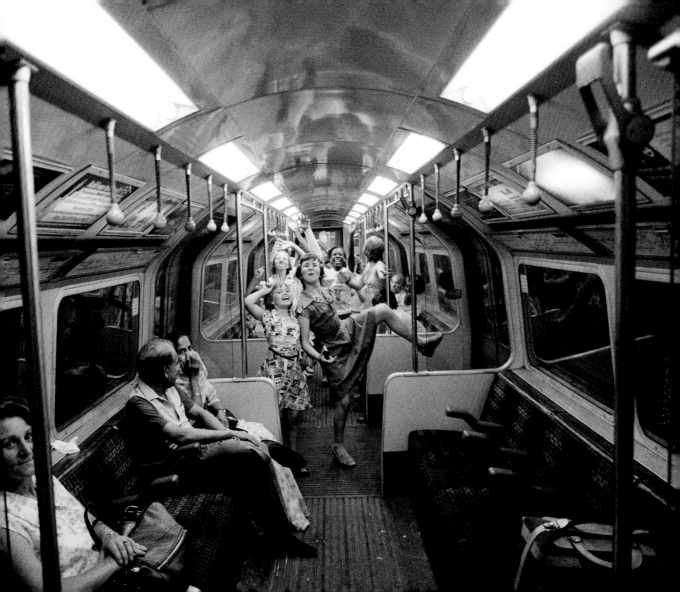

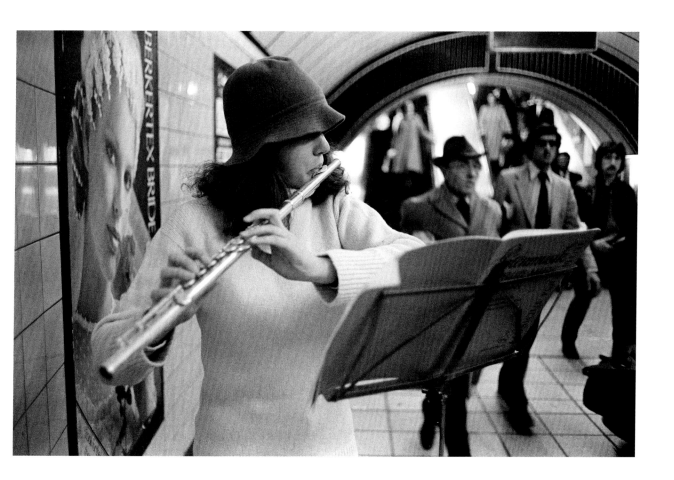

Oxford Circus, 1980

Wembley Park, 1979

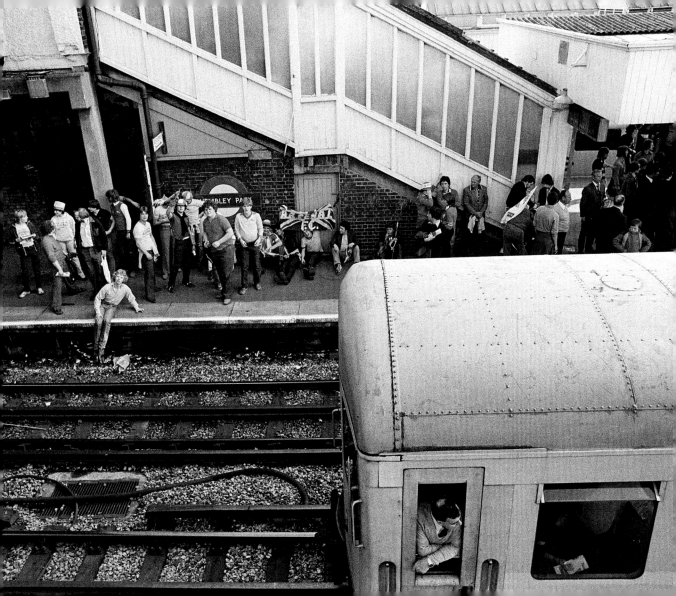

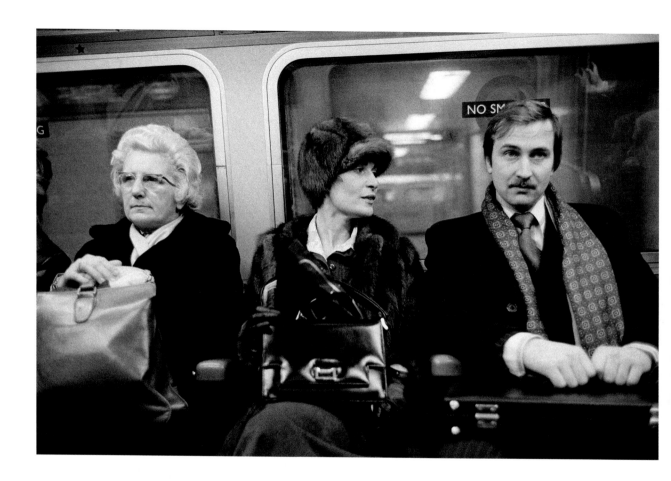

Victoria Line, 1980

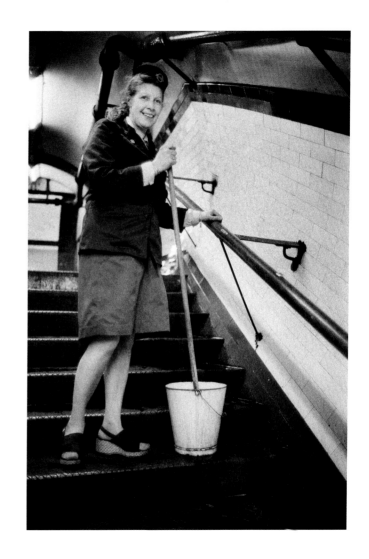

Chalk Farm, 1977

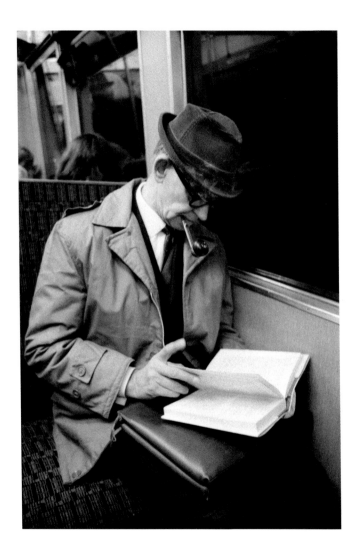

Metropolitan Line, 1977

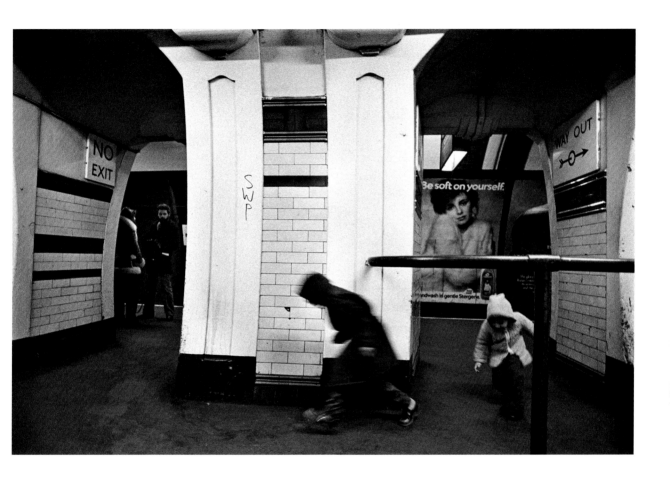

Monument, 1979

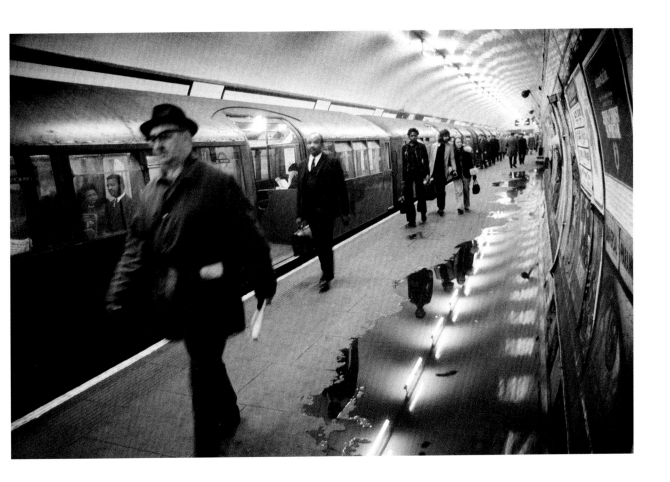

Chalk Farm, 1973

Bromley-by-Bow, 1975

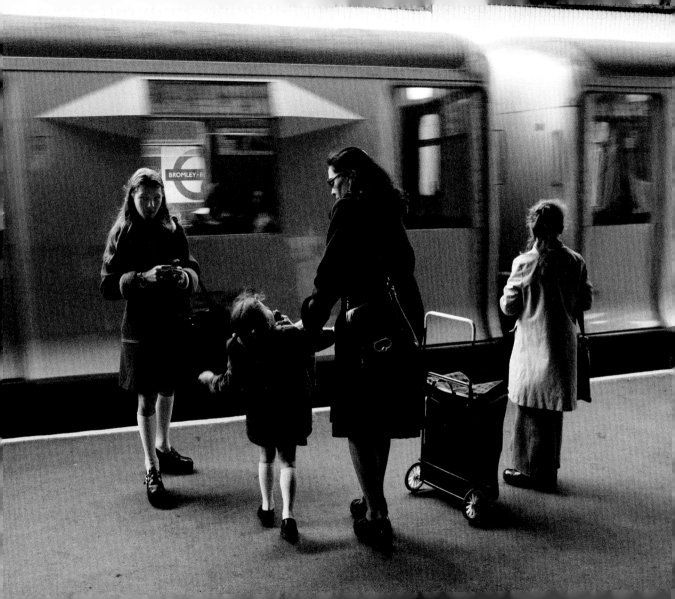

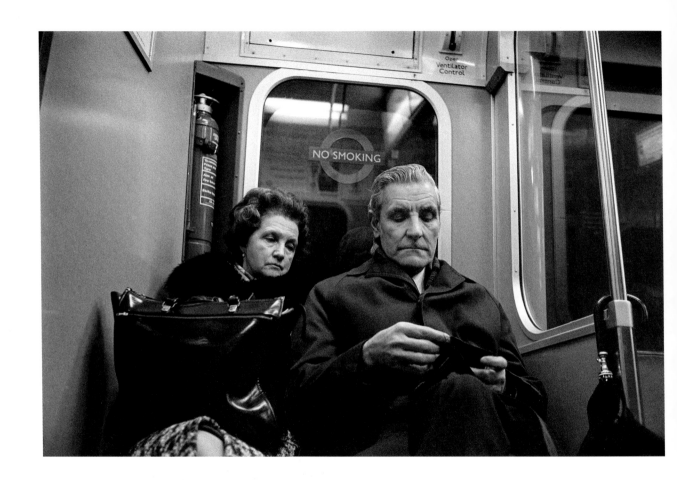

Circle Line, 1978

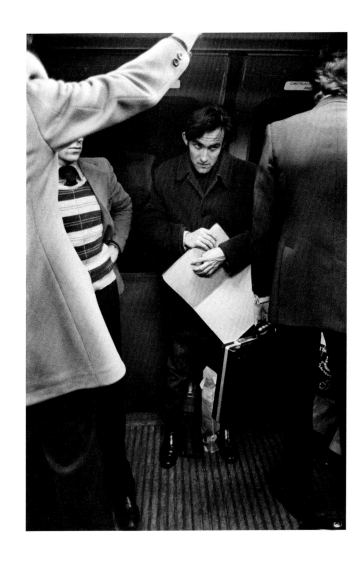

Central Line, 1972

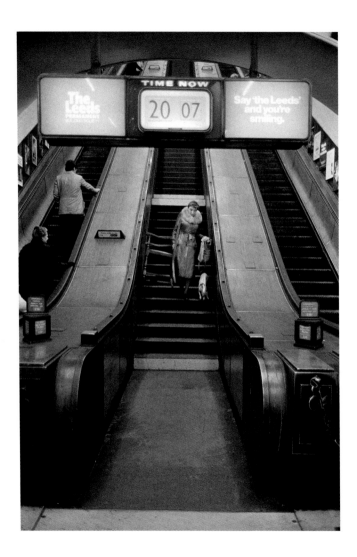

Knightsbridge, 1980

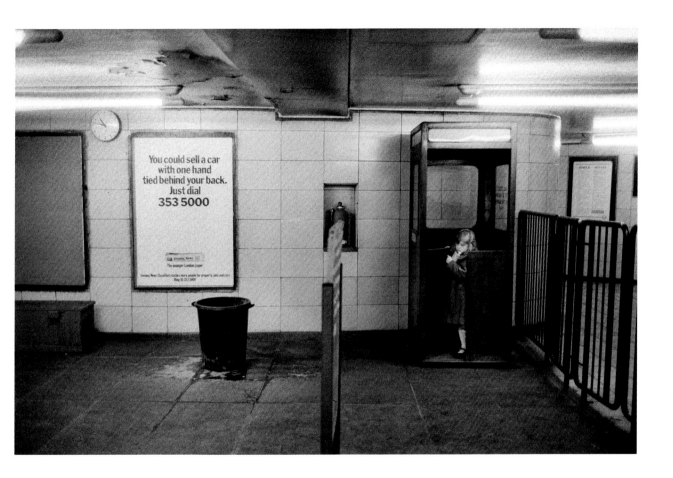

Bethnal Green, 1978

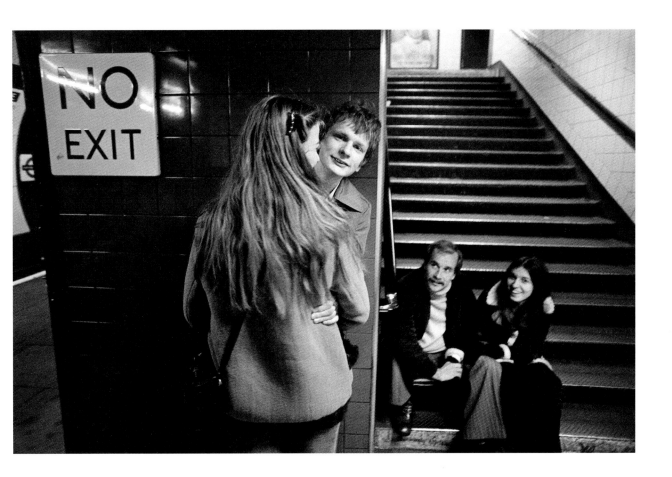

Oxford Circus, 1979

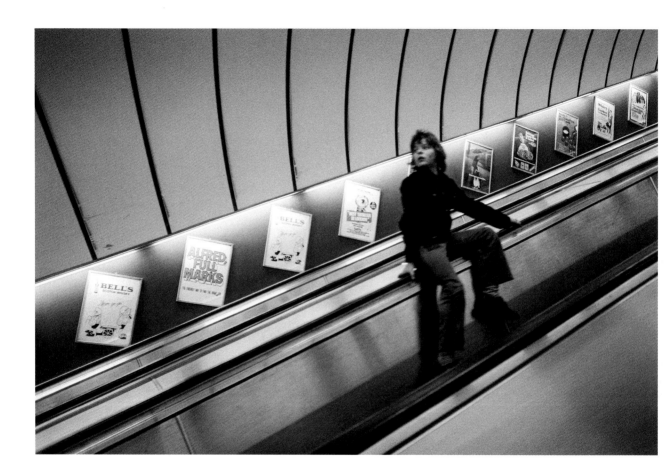

King's Cross, 1974

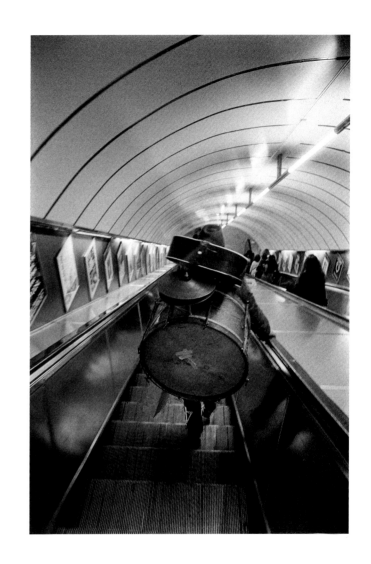

Oxford Circus, 1972

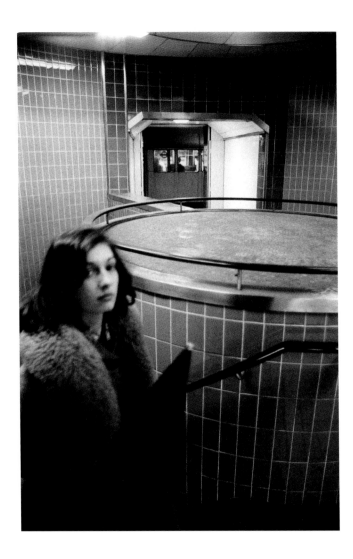

Bank, 1973

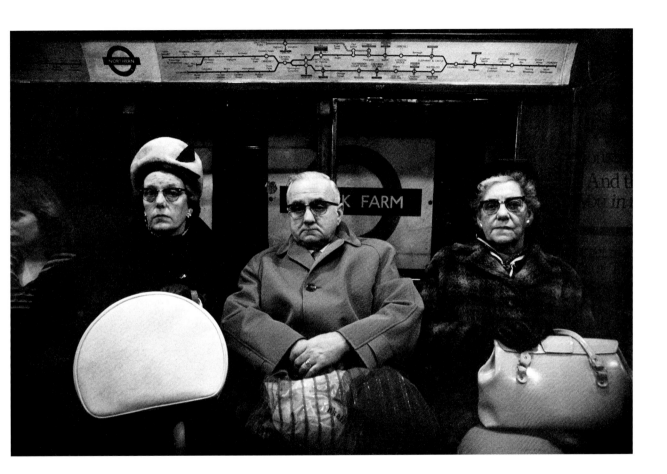

Northern Line, 1971

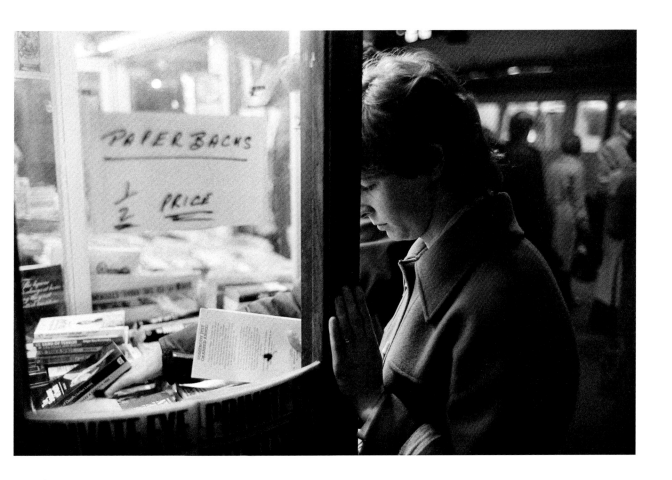

Baker Street, 1978

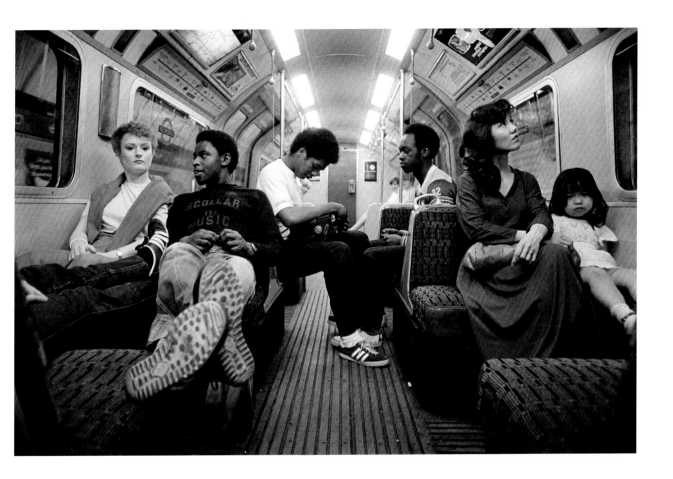

Victoria Line, 1979

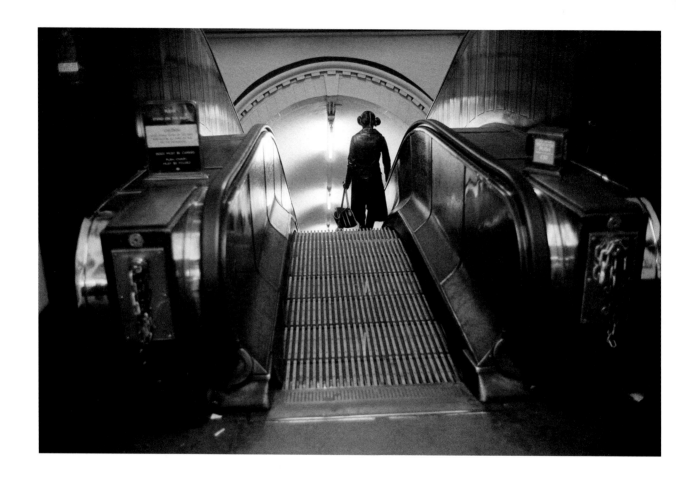

Embankment, 1978

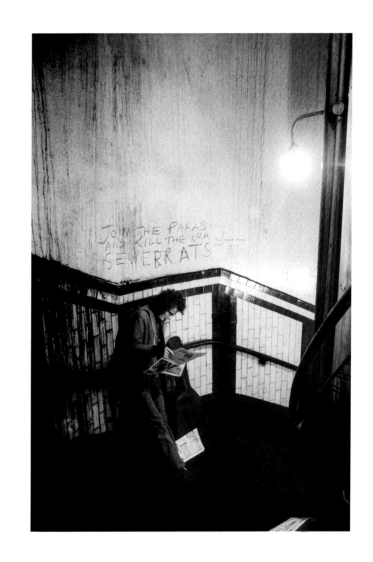

Belsize Park, 1970

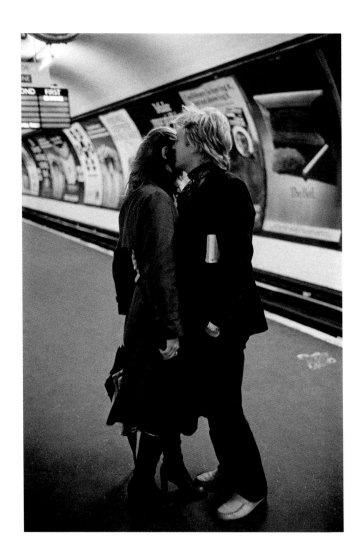

Bank, 1978

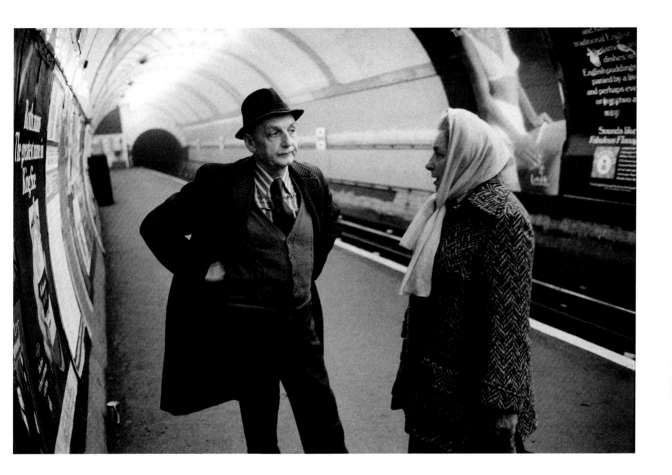

Camden Town, 1977

Tottenham Court Road, 1979

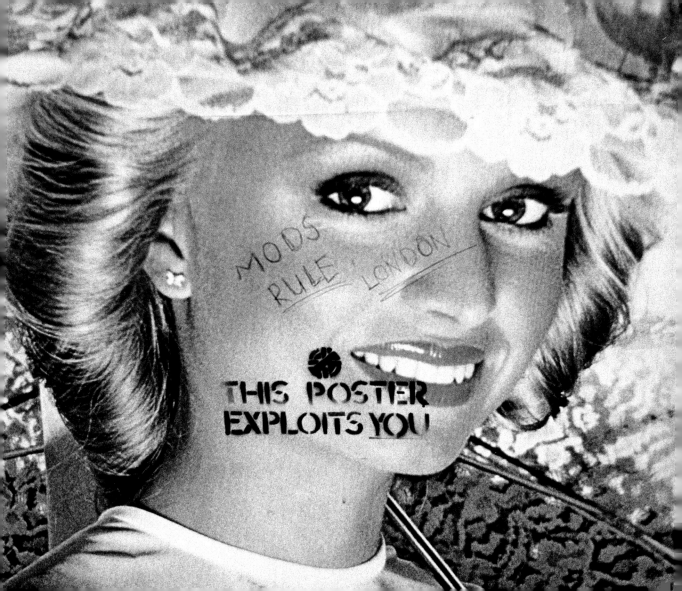

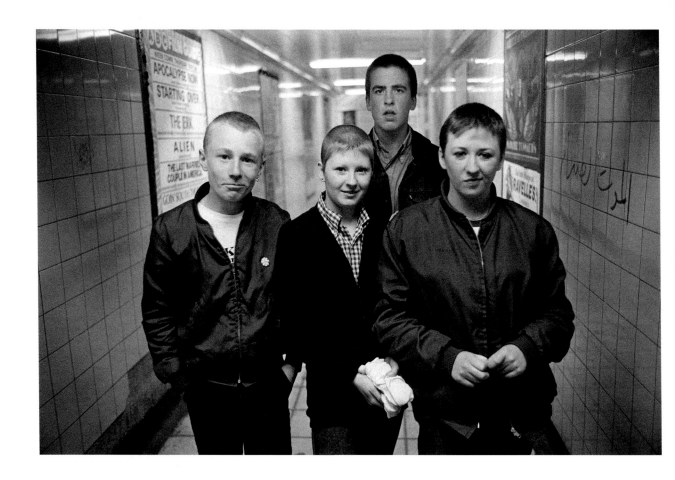

Tottenham Court Road, 1980

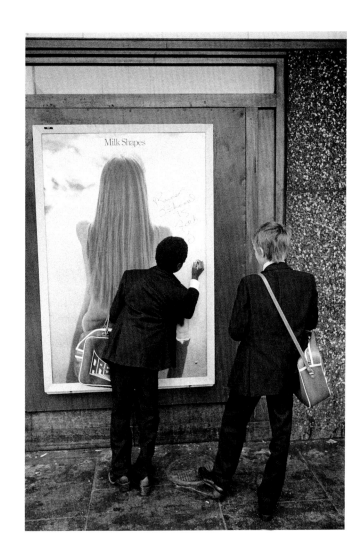

Kilburn Park, 1979

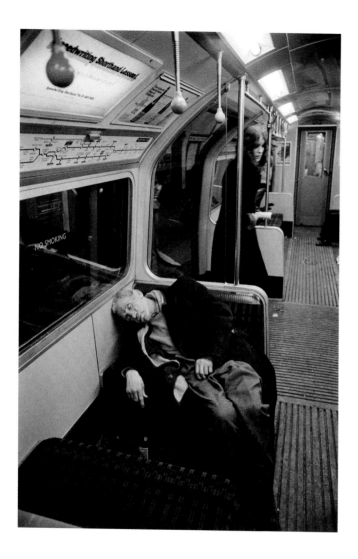

Northern Line, 1973

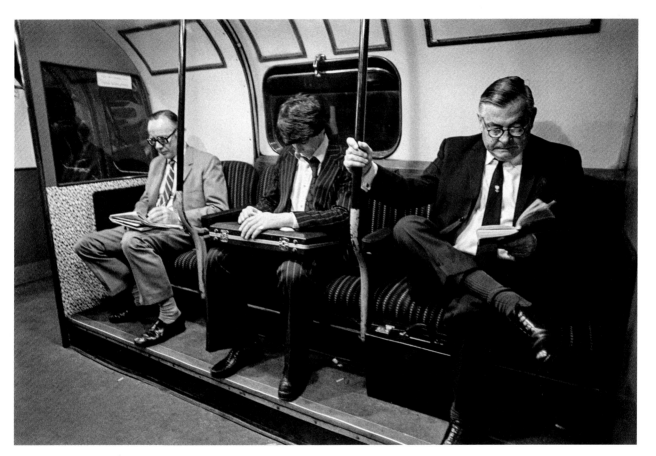

Waterloo & City Line, 1979

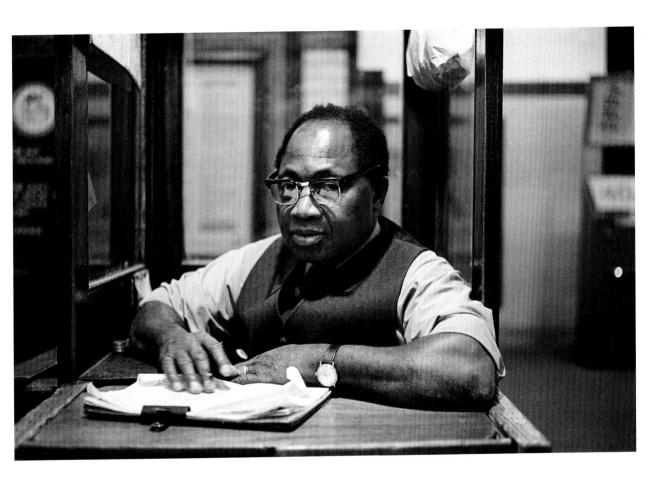

Golders Green, 1979

Farringdon, 1978

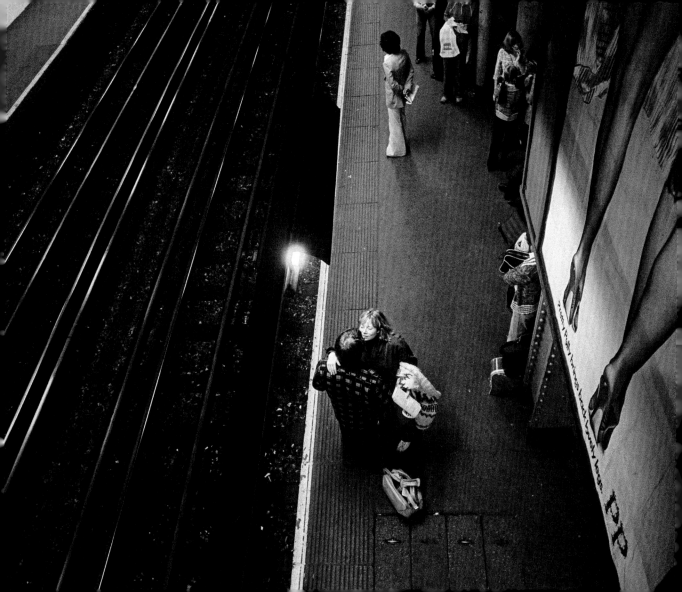

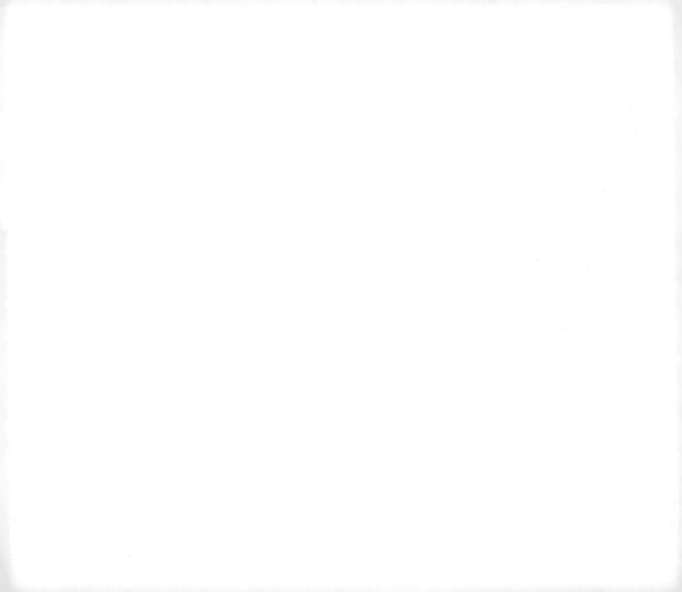

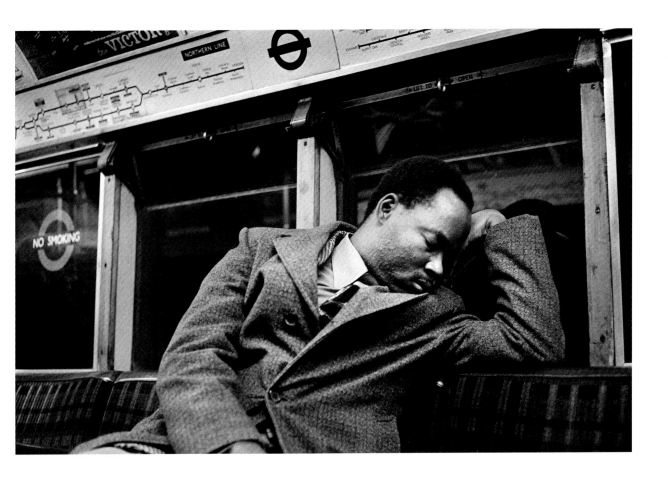

Northern Line, 1973

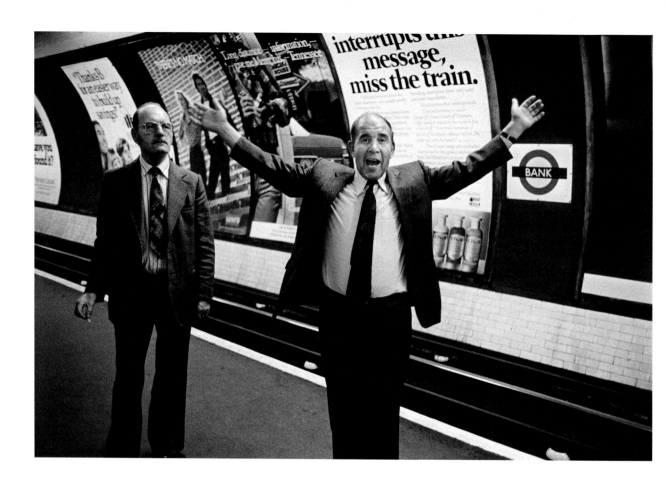

Bank, 1979

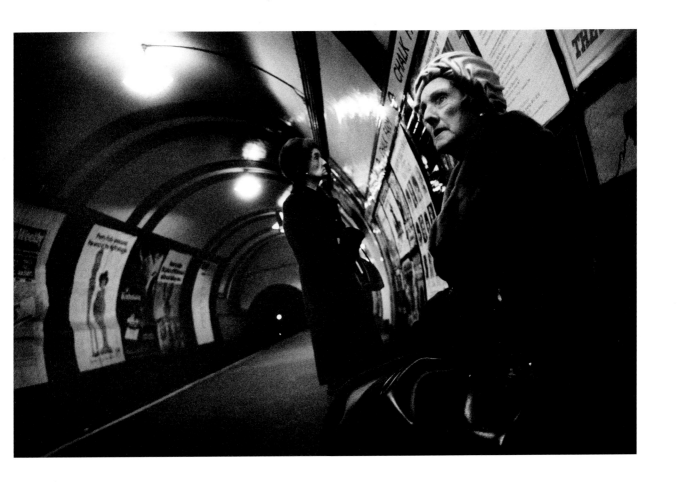

Chalk Farm, 1971

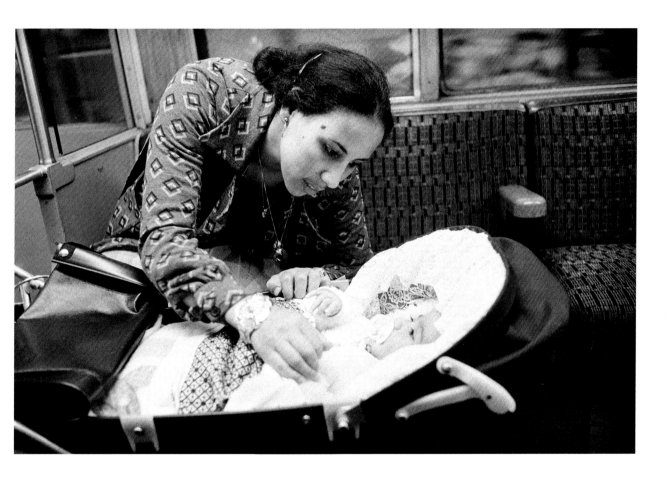

Northern Line, 1974

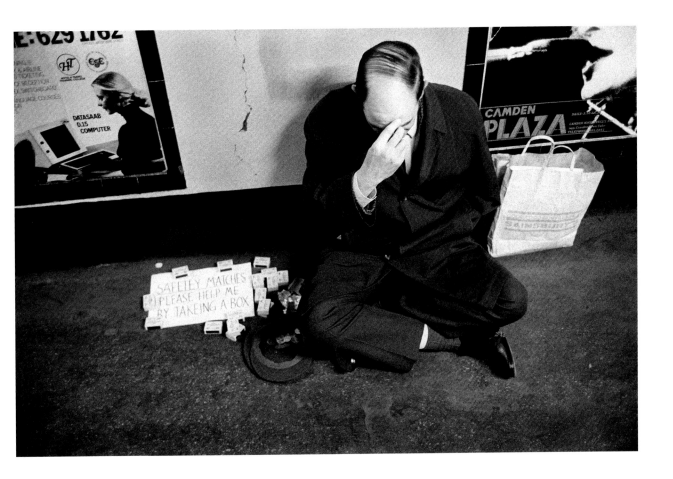

Tottenham Court Road, 1977

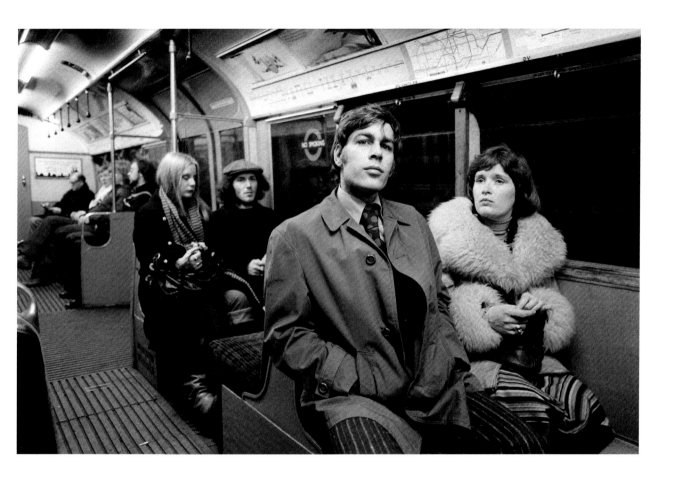

Piccadilly Line, 1975

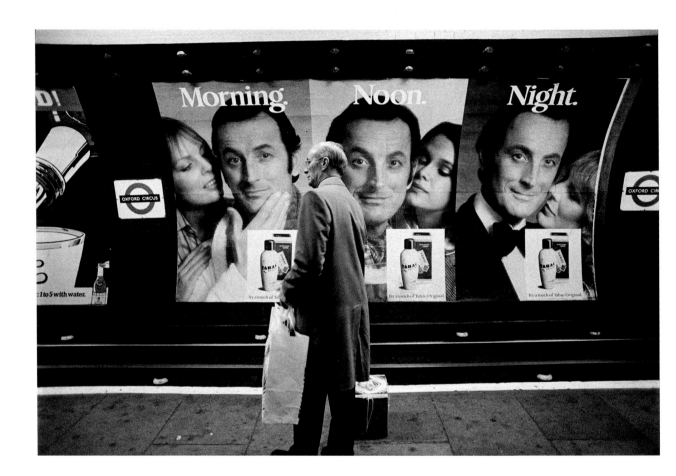

Oxford Circus, 1978

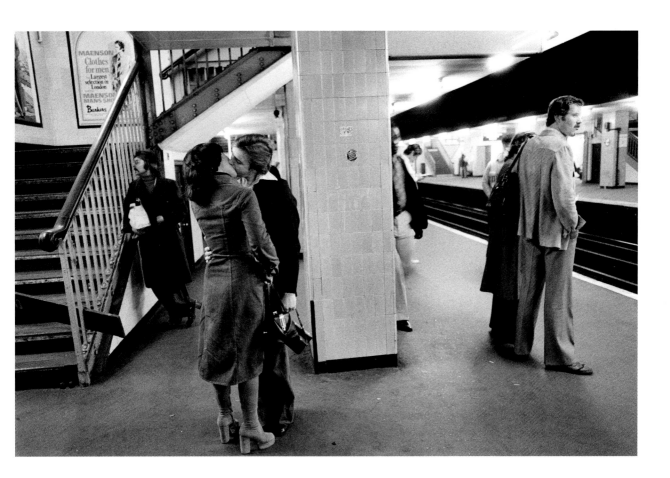

Moorgate, 1974

Embankment, 1974

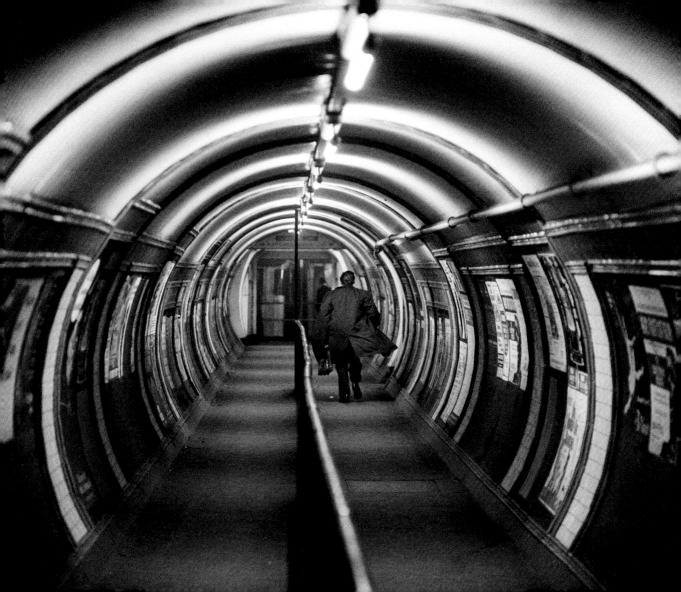

London Underground 1970–1980

For Wendy, Sam and Dan

First edition, second printing

Copyright © Hoxton Mini Press 2019. All rights reserved.
All photographs © Mike Goldwater
Introduction text by Lucy Davies
Design and sequence by Hoxton Mini Press and Mike Goldwater
Production, design and editorial support from
Anna De Pascale, Daniele Roa and Faith McAllister

Caption for image on p.4: Baker Street, 1979

ISBN: 978-1-910566-61-9

Printed and bound by Artron, China

To order books, collector's editions and signed prints, please go to:
www.hoxtonminipress.com

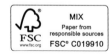

FSC
www.fsc.org
MIX
Paper from
responsible sources
FSC® C019910